Waking Up to Your Greatness

What would you say if I told you that having more money isn't so much about changing the way you work as much as it is changing the way you think? And what if I told you that you have the ability to make as much money as you want?

Would you say I was crazy? Off my rocker? Not making any sense?

I certainly understand that. After all, for our entire lives, we've been told that the only way to have more money is to either:

- Win the lottery
- Work harder

The odds of you winning the lottery are small – and besides, there's a much better way to make money.

And while there's certainly some truth that you must work hard if you want money, you can have as much money as you want without necessarily working harder.

Yes, for real!

See, here's the thing...

There's not a direct correlation between how hard you work and how much money you make.

Especially if you work for a salary. After all, you can work incredibly hard and only get a 3% raise every year.
No matter how hard you work...

...you're still going to be limited by your salary.

However, there is a direct correlation between your money mindset and how much money you make.

In other words, the way you think about money has a real and direct influence on how much money you actually make.

Your money mindset can either:

- Catapult you to wealth
- Keep you in poverty

That's how powerful it is.

This is why most people never reach the level of success they truly want. They don't have an effective mindset about achieving success and gaining wealth. They're trapped where they are and don't know how to change.

They've done things a certain way for so long that they can't see any other way of doing them.

In his book Secrets Of The Millionaire Mind, T. Harv Ecker says:

> The reality is that most people do not reach their full potential. Most people are not successful. Research shows that 80 percent of individuals will never be financially free in the way they'd like to be, and 80 percent will never claim to be truly happy. The reason is simple. Most people are unconscious. They are a little asleep at the wheel. They work and think on a superficial level of life—based only on what they can see. They live strictly in the visible world.

Does this describe you?

- Not reaching your full potential?
- Not financially free?
- Not truly happy?
- Asleep at the wheel?

You know that you should be achieving great things...

...but you just can t quite seem to get there.

Then this book is for you.

This book will teach you how to change your mind and truly change your life. It will blow up many of the myths that you've believed for years and help reshape your thinking.

The only prerequisite for reading this book is an open mind.

Some of what you're about to read may contradict beliefs you've held about yourself and money for years. These beliefs have been holding you back from reaching your true potential.

It's time for those beliefs to be put to rest and for you to embrace the true reality of who you are.

It's time to stop being unconscious - asleep at the wheel - and to wake up to your greatness.

Ready?

Let's get started.

Myths You've Believed About Money

There's a good chance that what you believe about money is simply wrong. We've been conditioned by society, by our parents, and by our friends to believe certain things about money.

And most of us have believed those things without EVER questioning them.

Again, to quote T. Harv Ecker:

> You were taught how to think and act when it comes to money. These teachings become your conditioning, which becomes automatic responses that run you for the rest of your life. Unless, of course, you intercede and revise your mind's money files.

As a result, we have what you might call a "difficult" relationship with money:

- *We want more of it* but can't ever seem to get enough.

- *We know that money can achieve good things*, but we feel conflicted when we spend it.

- *We're grateful when we have the money to purchase the things we want*, but also feel like we're being selfish.

Why do we have this relationship with money? Why do we get so tied up in knots over it? Why do we stress about it so much?

It's because we've believed a lot of myths and lies about money.

And we've never questioned our beliefs to see if they're actually true. And because we've never questioned them, we haven't achieved the level of success that we truly want.

In her book *You Are A Badass At Making Money*, Jen Sincero says:

> Our beliefs, along with our thoughts and words, are at the root of everything we experience in life, which is why consciously choosing what rolls around in your mind and falls out of your mouth is one of the most important things you can do. This conscious choosing of your thoughts, beliefs, and words is called mastering your mindset, and master it you must if you'd like to live large and in charge.

If you want more success, money, and happiness, then it's crucial that you stop believing money myths and master your mindset about money.

Mastering your money mindset requires dispelling the myths you've believed for so long.

Let's look at some of the common myths we've believed about money.

Money Myth #1: Money Is Evil

We've all heard it said that money is the root of all evil. Maybe your parents reinforced this myth when you were growing up. They didn't want to accumulate too much money because they were afraid that it would result in evil.

And so, you've unconsciously adopted this belief.

- You don't want to accumulate too much money because you're afraid of what it will do to you.

- You believe that somehow money will turn you evil.

- Or you believe that money itself is evil.

But is this true? Is money actually evil?

No.

Take a minute and think about what money actually is.

Money is simply printed paper. Or a chunk of metal, like a gold bar. Or just digital numbers in your bank account that go up and down.

Is that paper or metal inherently evil?

Nope.

Money itself is neutral. It's not good and it's not bad.

Think about it this way. When you put a $20 bill in your wallet, does that make you a worse person?

Of course not.
What if you put a $100 bill in your wallet?

You're still not a bad person.

That's because money itself is not evil. It's morally neutral.

Adding more money to your bank account doesn't mean that you're somehow adding something bad to your life. You're simply adding more numbers to your account.

Here's the key point: It's what you do with money, not money itself, that is good and bad.

- You can do great good with money.
- You can give it to people in need.
- You can buy something for yourself that you really want.
- You can start a charity.
- You can help your friend start a business.

And, of course, you can also do bad things with money.

You get the point. It's the actions you take, not money itself, that is evil.

So let's put this myth to bed. Money is neutral, not evil.

Myth #2: People Who Want Money Are Greedy

Many of us carry around the assumption that only people who are greedy want more money. We assume that if we want money, we'll become like Ebenezer Scrooge, always hoarding money but never giving it away.

But is this true?

No.

Again, money is a neutral thing. It's what you do with money that truly matters.

So yes, you can be greedy and simply want to accumulate as much money as possible.

But having more money also allows you to be extremely generous. It allows you to give good things to others. It allows you to donate to charity.

You simply can't do those things if you don't have money.

Did you catch that?

You can t be generous if you don t have money.

Think about that for a minute.

If you want to be financially generous, you have to have some finances in the first place.

It's time to kill this myth. Wanting more money does not make you greedy.

Myth #3: There Is Not Enough Money

If you grew up in a house where finances were regularly "tight", then you may harbor the belief that there is not enough money.

You believe that the reason you don't have enough money is because there simply isn't enough money to go around.

But let's step back a minute and evaluate this belief.

How much money is in the world?

Trillions and trillions of dollars.

There is more than enough money for everyone. There is not a scarcity of money.

In fact, there is an actual abundance of money in the world.

Just because you don't have all the money that you want doesn't mean that there's not enough money.

This is the difference between a "scarcity" mindset and an "abundance" mindset:

- *With a scarcity mindset, you believe that there is never enough.* You feel like you have to hold onto everything you have because you never know when it will be gone.

- *With an abundance mindset, you believe that there is more than enough for everyone.* When you get money, it doesn't mean that someone else is not getting money.

So, as you see, *money is not a zero-sum game.* In other words, you receiving money does not mean that someone else is losing money.

That's not how it works.

There is more than enough money in the world for everyone to have as much as they want.

Let's kill this myth. There's plenty for everyone. We live in a world of abundance.

Myth #4: I'll Never Make Enough Money

If you believe that you'll never make enough money, then you certainly will never make enough money.

But why do you have that belief in the first place?

If there is more than enough money in the world for everyone, why should you believe that you'll never make enough?

You're an incredibly talented person that has so much to offer the world, and it's critical that you believe that. Your skills, talents, and expertise are worth money, and there are lots of people out there who are willing to pay for those skills.

But in order for this to be your reality, you have to believe it first.

You have to stop buying into the lie that you'll never make enough money and start affirming that you are going to make more than you could imagine.

You may not know exactly how you're going to make the money, but that's okay.

You have to master your mindset, and that means having the unshakeable belief that you're going to increase your income.

Let's kick this myth to the curb. You can and will make more than enough money if you're willing to believe it first.

Myth #5: If I Make More Money, People Won't Like Me

This is a common myth that many people believe, especially if their parents didn't like people who had money.

But the reality is we don t dislike people who make money. We dislike people who flaunt their wealth in an arrogant way.

Again, this goes back to how you use your money.

If you make more money and then start bragging to your friends about how awesome you are, then sure, they might not like you anymore.

But if you use your increased income to help others, people will actually like you more! And they certainly won't begrudge you for spending some on yourself.

This myth needs to go far away. As long as you don't flaunt your wealth in an annoying, arrogant way, you'll be just fine. In fact, people will probably appreciate you more as you accumulate wealth.

Myth #6: I'm Just Fine Without Money

If you've struggled for a long time to achieve financial stability, then you may have convinced yourself that you're just fine without having any money.

But is this really true?

- Are you really living your absolute best life?
- Are you the best version of yourself that you can be?
- Are you able to live fearlessly, generously, and joyfully?

Let's be honest: money makes many things possible that aren't possible otherwise.

Money allows you to expand your horizons by traveling the world. It allows you to deepen friendships by going out to dinner with your close friends. It allows you to support worthy causes.

If you don't have money, you can't expand into your full potential. You can't be your best self.

To be clear, I'm not saying that people without money are somehow defective. That's wrong thinking. I'm simply saying that money gives you options that you wouldn't have otherwise.

Let's be done with this myth. *It's time for you to achieve your true greatness.*

The Power of Your Mind: Having an Abundance Mindset

Your mind is an incredibly powerful thing. Far more powerful than you can even imagine.

What you think about has an incredible effect on the quality of your life and whether you reach your dreams. In fact, your brain controls most of your reality:

- What you think about...
- What you give your attention to...
- What you focus on...

...literally controls the outcomes in your life.

Marcus Aurelius said:

> The happiness of your life depends upon the quality of your thoughts.

Therefore, guard accordingly, and take care that you entertain no notions unsuitable to virtue and reasonable nature.

This is true. The happiness of your life and the reality you create depends primarily upon your thoughts. That's how powerful your brain is.

If you want to be happy and attract wealth, it's crucial to adopt a certain mindset.

You must have a mindset of abundance.

Because of this, it's absolutely essential that we learn to master the way we think about wealth and abundance.

Your Mind Controls Your Outcomes

What most people fail to realize is that their mind creates almost all of the outcomes in their lives. Every outcome you're experiencing right now, whether it's positive or negative, is primarily the result of your thoughts.

Or, to put it another way, what you constantly think about shapes your reality.

Your focus determines what you attract:

- Focus on positive things and you'll attract positive things.
- Focus on negative things and you'll attract the negative.

Yes, your mind really is that powerful. Again, as Jen Sincero says:

> ...we can literally create the reality we desire by making ourselves think and believe what we desire to think and believe. How awesome is that?!

Or as T. Harv Ecker puts it:

> Whatever results you're getting, be they rich or poor, good or bad, positive or negative, always remember that your outer world is simply a reflection of your inner world. If things aren't going well in your outer life, it's because things aren't going well in your inner life. It's that simple.

Are you starting to get the picture? As Ecker says, your outer world (reality) is simply a reflection of your inner world (your thoughts, desires, and dreams).

If you're not experiencing what you want in your life, it's primarily due to what's happening in your inner world.

- Not attracting the wealth you want? Inner world.
- Not able to get your head above water financially? Inner world.
- Not able to move forward in your job like you should? Inner world.

The good news is that you are the one in control of your inner world.

You determine what you think about and focus on. The more you control and shape your inner world, the more you will control and shape your actual reality.

Isn't that amazing to think about?

The massive implication is that if you want to change your life and attract more wealth, you absolutely must master the way you think.

Changing Your Mind About Money

If your outer world is a reflection of your inner world, then it's absolutely essential that you master your mindset about money. You need to be done with the myths from your past and adopt an abundance mindset.

If you have a scarcity mindset, believing that there is never enough money, then that is exactly what you will attract into your life. You will attract scarcity. You attract exactly what you focus on.

But if you believe in the abundance of the world, you'll attract abundance into your life. If you believe that there is more than enough for you and everyone else, you'll begin manifesting that in your life.
What you believe becomes your reality.

Therefore, it's important to believe:

- There's enough money for everyone.
- You simply need to reach out and take it.

Think about all the abundance in the world. You simply need to open yourself up to receive it.

Whether you believe in God or universal intelligence or the energy behind all things, you must believe that it wants you to have money. Because it really does.

The world is full of abundance, and if you're living in scarcity, then you're not enjoying all that the world has to offer.

It's time to change your mind about money. To believe that there's enough, that you deserve to have money, and that you were created to experience abundance.

Regularly affirm this. Tell yourself these things over and over again until they're burned into your brain. Until you believe them with all your heart and soul.

Opportunities Are Everywhere

Once you start having an abundance mindset and open yourself up to all that the Creator wants to give you, you'll start seeing opportunities everywhere.

- You'll see ways to acquire money that you never would have seen before.

- Opportunities will drop into your lap out of nowhere.

- You'll begin to attract money in ways that surprise you.

But you must open your mind to the possibilities that are all around you. The world is full of infinite possibilities, and just because you can't see them doesn't mean they're not there.

Angelina Zimmerman puts it this way:

> The scarcity pathway leads one to experience a life not fully lived, a life that can only be described as pedestrian. Overflowing with strong negative reactions like the high tide that creates waves in a rock pool not to mention the countless missed opportunities and experiences.
>
> Those that choose to walk along the path of abundance experience a completely different life. Opting to live life to the full, exuding happiness, generous by nature, creative and inspirational. Taking full advantage and enjoying the wave of opportunities that come their way, along with memorable experiences.

Today, choose the path of abundance.

One of the best ways to choose abundance is through the practice of gratitude.

Start practicing gratitude for all the ways that the Creator has got your back and is bringing abundance into your life. When you receive something good and positive, say a simple, "Thank you." This practice will start to transform the way you live.

When you're grateful for even the smallest things, it puts positive energy out into the world, which then attracts more positive things into your life.

It really is a powerful cycle. You put out the positive energy of gratitude and you are rewarded with more things to be grateful for.

Amazing, isn't it?

So, begin practicing gratitude immediately. As you shift your mindset from scarcity to abundance, you'll be shocked by all the good things that start to come into your life.

Taking Action on Your Dreams

And abundance mindset is absolutely necessary if you want to attract wealth and build your dreams.

But an abundance mindset alone is not enough.

ACTION is needed.

You must start taking action on your dreams.

When you have an abundance mindset and you start taking action on your dreams...

...you truly do become limitless.

There is absolutely nothing that can stop you. You will achieve more than you thought possible.

In other words, you may have an abundance mindset, but if you don't start taking action on your dreams, nothing will change. However, abundance mindset combined with action leads to great things.

The equation is:

Abundance + Action = Dreams Become Reality

Once you start taking action, you'll begin to see the things you dreamed about becoming an actual reality.

Isn't that exciting to think about? Doesn't that get you fired up?

When taking action on your dreams, follow these steps...

Step #1: Write Your Dreams Down

The first step is to write down your dreams and goals. Be as specific as possible when writing them down. You want to be so specific that you can see them in your mind's eye.

Ask yourself questions like:

- What do I want to get out of life?
- What are my biggest dreams?
- What do I want to accomplish?
- How much money do I want to make?
- When do I want to make it by?

The more concrete you can be when writing down your dreams and goals, the more you'll be able to visualize them coming true.

The more you can visualize them, the more positive emotion you'll feel around them and the more focused you'll be on them.

And the more focused you are on your dreams, the more you'll attract them into your life.

It's really that simple.

T. Harv Ecker calls this the wealth principle:

> **WEALTH PRINCIPLE:**
> *Thoughts lead to feelings. Feelings lead to actions. Actions lead to results.*

So, write down your dreams and goals with as many details as possible. Feel them intensely. Feel how amazing it will be when you accomplish them.

These feelings will lead to actions, which will then translate into absolutely amazing results.

After you've written down your dreams, rehearse them again and again. Repeat them to yourself every single day. Affirm that they are going to come true.

Say things like:

- "I affirm that I am going to double my income by XX date."
- "I affirm that I am a financial success in all areas of my life."
- "I affirm that I will break the company sales record this year."
- "I affirm that this is my best year ever financially."

Repeat these affirmations again and again until you believe with all your heart that they're true.

Raise your energy level and feelings around these affirmations until you're ready to take big actions on them.

Even if you don't know how these things are going to happen, affirm that they will. These kinds of affirmations create positive energy around you that will keep you motivated and on track.

As Gary John Bishop says:

> ...the person who views success as if it were just around the corner will not only work his butt off to achieve it but be energized and alive to it all the while acting on that fundamental view [abundance] of success....You see, our thoughts are so powerful that they are constantly pushing you toward your goals, even when you don't realize what those goals actually are! Your brain is wired to win.

Plus, the energy that you put out into the world comes back to you.

If you put out positive energy in the form of affirmations and gratitude, you'll see that positive energy coming back to you in positive forms.

Step #2: Start Taking Action on Your Dreams

Once you've written down your dreams and begun to rehearse them each day, it's crucial to start taking action.

Map out what specific steps you need to follow in order to achieve your dreams, and then begin taking those actions.

What do you need to do in order to make your dreams a reality? Don't worry if you don't have this all figured out. Just begin taking action on whatever comes to mind.

- Do you need to call someone?
- Hire a mentor?
- Start building another business on the side?
- Send an email to an important contact?

- Call a friend you haven't spoken to in a while?

If you have an abundance mindset and are open to new opportunities, actions will begin to pop into your mind. You'll start to have ideas that you didn't have before.

Take action on these ideas. These are cues that are intended to guide you on the path to wealth and success.

Make it your goal to take action on your dreams every single day. To move at least a little bit closer to achieving what you truly want.

When something comes to your mind, take action on it.

The more you take action, the more impressive the results you'll see. You'll realize that you truly do have limitless potential. You'll achieve things you never believed were possible.

Your Dreams Are Waiting for You

And now for the million-dollar question: *what are you going to do with your life?*

You now know that:

- You truly have limitless potential.
- Most of the myths you've believed about money are totally false.
- Your inner thoughts control your outer reality.
- You have the power to shape your reality.
- You can attract and manifest the wealth and dreams that you desire.
- The Creator totally has your back and is supporting your dreams.

Are you going to start taking action on your dreams? Or are you going to continue living asleep at the wheel, walking through life mostly unconscious?

Are you going to take control of your destiny, master your money mindset, and achieve your dreams, or are you going to continue struggling?

There is an amazing future out there, just waiting for you to seize it. Don't let that future pass you by. Don't arrive 30 years from now and regret the actions that you didn't take.

Master your money mindset today and watch what begins to happen. You'll be absolutely floored by the results!

EXCLUSIVE OFFER

You took action to take control of your income and future, and for that I want to give you an exclusive offer only available to those who purchase this book.

There is much work ahead to get your business launched, and I want to help you get there.

That is why I developed the Secret Success Mindset Masterclass: How the Most Successful Achieve the Unimaginable.

Below is a coupon code for you to get 50% off this training.

BONUS: When you purchase the training using the code below, you will also receive a complimentary coaching call where I will help you set goals and milestones to ensure
your success.

Register at:
masterclass.getmindmagnet.com

Use Code: mmbook

www.ingramcontent.com/pod-product-compliance
Lightning Source LLC
Chambersburg PA
CBHW070802050426
42452CB00012B/2457